"Finally a book that shows the

TRUST ME, I'M A SALESMAN

How to Earn Customers through Trust and Value

YURI VAN DER SLUIS

Trust Me, I'm a Salesman

First Edition
ISBN 978-988-78901-0-2
Published in Hong Kong

All of the characters and events in this book are fictitious. Any similarity you may find however with actual sales people is not coincidental and intended by the author.

Publisher: YuTrain Ltd
Front cover Image by: INK Strategy
Interior artwork by: INK Strategy
Translated and edited by: Joy Philips
Interior Design: Heidi North

Ordering information:
Special Discounts are available on large quantity purchases by corporations, associations, and others. For details contact the publisher at info@yutrain.com

www.topsalesdogs.com
www.yurivander.com

10 9 8 7 6 5 4 3 2 1

Do you want to substantially grow your business?

How the battlefield of selling looks today

Today, customers have no time, have plenty of potential suppliers at their disposal, and little patience to learn about you and what you can offer. For sales people, they have even less tolerance. They simply don't trust you. Their bad experiences from the past, or even from today, are standing between you and your customer. The ever-increasing number of sellers offering their products and services to potential customers only increases this "trust gap".

Why trust is the most powerful strategy that you can apply?

Without trust, without customer's openness, you won't be able to strategize, making your sales guesswork which is a far cry from mastery. You risk struggling every step of the way, without any predictability of whether you will close the deal, let alone make a healthy profit from it.

The good news is that trust is something which you can acquire and create with your customer. Just imagine what you could achieve if your customers would trust you blindly. You can set yourself apart from the mediocre sales people.

With the earned trust, you can have real conversations which matter and, most importantly, you can turn this trust into real contracts.

When you successfully apply the Top Sales Dog mindset, your customer will:

- Truly listen and engage with you
- Introduce you to their network
- Gladly pay you a higher price
- Follow your advice
- Open the door for you
- Make time for you
- Connect with you on social platforms and empower you
- Share sensitive information that nobody else knows
- Help you to prepare
- Quickly respond to your messages
- Be open and honest
- Battle for you
- Warn you about potential deal breakers
- Share competitive information to your advantage
- Be a reliable ally in business
- Help you close the deal
- Negotiate less
- Accept your proposal faster
- Forgive you for mistakes faster and easier
- Give you plenty other advantages

This book shows, in every step of the sales process, what the perfect mindset is to fully align yourself with your customer and increase that level of trust, which you know will result into performance levels that you can't obtain in any other way.

Remember:

"YOU CAN'T PUSH TRUST, YOU CAN ONLY EARN IT"

CONTENTS

Needless to say, this book addresses both men and women. Don't let the title or illustrations fool you; sales professionals come in all stripes, shapes, shades and genders, and the aim of this book is absolutely inclusive. If you're in sales, this book is for you.

Acknowledgments

Trust Me, I'm a Salesman would not have been possible without the help, support, and inspiring talents of many wonderful people:

• My wife, Emily, who had to endure my crazy writing hours and who pushed and supported me throughout the entire creative and writing process. I would have never finished this project without her.
• My personal friend, mentor and life coach, Nathan Kotek, owner of themessagebuilder.com, the unique and amazing messaging expert, who helped me to focus and get the right messages out.
• The incredible visual designers at INK Strategy, who truly demonstrated their talent by translating my thoughts into striking visuals.
• My toughest critic, friend, and amazing entrepreneur, Brahim Samhoud owner of BNZSA, who was always ready to point out the weak spots that required improvements.
• Gurus who have inspired me throughout my sales career — Seth Godin, Simon Sinek, Michael T. Bosworth, Neil Rackham, William Skip Miller, Alen Mayer, Ari Galper, Daniel Pink, and Sharon Drew Morgen.
• Some of my most important partners, whom I have been working very closely with and were able to implement sales methodologies within many IT companies — Remco Rijnhart, Juri Pietersen, Menno Zorn, and Johanan Bos — all of whom are part of the IT Channel Company.
• John Numan, who has guided me and helped to get the very first Dutch version of Trust me, I'm a Salesman published for the Dutch market.
• Invaluable no-nonsense guidance from Jacob Nayman, the author of the best seller in the field of wealth management, "The 1%".
• All my clients and their customer-centric sales professionals, who have taught me more about the right approach to sales than I could have ever experienced by myself.
• You, my readers, supporters of the Top Sales Dog approach and those spreading the word. If you ever have a question or suggestion, send me an email: yuri@topsalesdogs.com
• And, lastly, all those primitive, traditional poor sales role models, who put themselves and wallets as the centerpiece of the world, demonstrating what sales should not be about.

*"Selling is adding value to the customer,
and getting paid for it as a reward"*
- Yuri van der Sluis

A DREAM FOR THE FUTURE

My dream is to see sales professionals earn good money without being greedy. I'd like to see people pitch their product from a place of inspiration and pride, only offering solutions that serve the customer's needs – and that you can definitely deliver. I dream of only closing deals if we really know our customers inside and out and are sure we can help them move forward. I'd like to see sales soar not because our salespeople cut corners, but because our customers are so intensely satisfied that they encourage everyone they've ever met to try our products and services.

When companies put customers first, we can all work together to contribute to a better society, based on values like loyalty, trust and intrinsic value, rather than relying on deception and greed. In the society I dream of, we would not have to push customers to buy. Instead, we should take pride in the way we sell, because we know that we're dedicated to benefiting our customers and improving the entire market.

As an advisor to the managing board, I've spent over ten years helping various sales and marketing organizations eliminate barriers to achieve sustainable commercial success. I integrate renowned business strategies with a range of my own methods developed in hands-on practice, transforming organizational limitations into a powerful capacity to inspire customer loyalty and connecting with customers on an exceptional level. I look at how they transpose their mission into their business model, their channels of distribution, their sales strategy, their brand promise, their reward system and their sales process – and I look at their ability to transform the way they think and act.

My aim is to encourage you to start the journey toward a more satisfying and effective way to sell—keeping the interests of the customer front and center. This book will contribute to a mindset of building trust and value. If you want to achieve real change, you need a practical and simple framework to follow. What I provide you with in this book are playful sales scenario cartoons, all intended to make you more conscious of your own behavior in the sales process. I compare the behavior of the wolf with that of the dog—an imaginary metaphor of two extremes used to emphasize differences in behavior, and to let you choose who you want to be. I hope this book will give you a new perspective and inspiration for how best to act in various sales scenarios throughout the entire buy cycle, based on a new mindset that makes both you and your client winners.

This book would never have been possible without the extensive, in-depth interactions with board members, sales managers and sales staff who shared their dilemmas, first-hand experiences and personal solutions with me. I sincerely hope that you'll be inspired to choose value over money and truly put your customers first. That's how the true sales professional comes into his own.

If sellers and buyers are able to trust each other again, we'll achieve so much more than we even imagine could be possible. Everyone has an opportunity: we can embrace our talents and responsibilities and use them to maximize value for our customers, our companies and ourselves. We can bring out the best in the profession. Are you ready to embrace your best self and help make the world a better place?

WHERE ARE THE SALES PROFESSIONALS?

It's fine to sell things, but specializing in sales seems less legit... and so there are no sales professionals. We see vice-presidents, directors, account managers, consultants, product managers, advisors, sales representatives and entrepreneurs: a whole crowd of people dedicated to helping customers make their purchases more effectively. But salespeople? No. They're there, of course; we just avoid calling them that. In a culture dominated by trade and commerce, you'd think that selling would be second nature – but we're not allowed to say it. We sell things, but we prefer to avoid actually admitting it.

And no wonder. If I ask you to describe a stereotypical salesman (just take a moment to think about it before you continue), you're probably imagining a fawning, irritating, pushy, unreliable character, an obsequious wheeler and dealer hiding their absent conscience behind a fake smile, out to part you from your hard-earned cash.

I have over fifteen years of experience in sales and have been training sales staff for ten years, and I've always wondered why the stereotypical salesman ended up being associated with that 'shady dealer', making everyone think that selling is a bad thing. The way things work now, salespeople are expected to be ashamed of their profession – but they shouldn't have to. Many sales professionals really are reliable, and it's time they got better publicity. Although these ethical sales experts don't hog the spotlight, they're much more effective, more skilled and more capable than those loud-mouthed swindlers. It's time for us to take a good, hard look at those two extremes and reassess the value of the salesman, the world's oldest and best profession.

So how can you be a successful sales professional, but still be proud of how you sell your products and services? In this book, I group sales professionals into two categories: wolves and dogs. The wolf devours his customers whole, gobbling them down, casting aside the scraps, and pouncing on the next victim without a moment's pause. The dog, in contrast, stays by his customer's side to ensure maximum value for the customer – not because it's expected of him, but because the dog believes it's important.

If you're reluctant to call yourself a sales professional because you loathe the way wolves behave, it's time to realize that you can also sell your products and services like a dog. If you recognize wolf behavior in yourself, be aware that your success may be short-lived. Wolves aren't worrying about the long term; they're too caught up in chasing short-term wins. The wolf proclaims loudly that you can trust him; the dog simply buckles down and proves it. If you were the customer, which of the two would you rather do business with? That's right! You'd have to be pretty masochistic to go for the wolf...

The wolf is a familiar figure from movies like Boiler Room and The Wolf of Wall Street. Sure, they're entertaining on the silver screen, and some parts are hilarious – but would you hand over YOUR hard-earned cash to unscrupulous salesmen like that? And if your company were on the market for a new security solution to handle your company's most sensitive data, would you want to work with those guys? And how about if you need a lawyer to arrange contract negotiations? I could continue, but enough with the introductions. Let's meet the wolf and the dog and discover the difference. Enjoy!

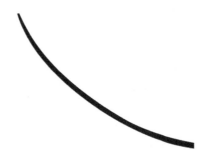

The SIP -- Sales Identity Paradox

The wolf is opportunistic, cunning and solely focused on the deal. So does that make the wolf the true sales professional? Not at all! No one actually wants to do business with a wolf. Ask a customer what they're looking for in a sales professional, and they'll describe someone who's honest, straightforward, and brainstorms with them to find solutions – and those salespeople are a crucial part of modern commerce. What would happen if all the sales professionals vanished overnight? Who would sell electric cars, raise funds for charity, convince people to buy recyclable products, help companies fund new medicines to treat rare diseases, or simply provide good products? The world needs sales dogs: people who are loyal and honest, who know how to create added value and are constantly working to make things better. Those are the sales professionals that people want to work with – and those are the people who will be ideally positioned to sell the concepts that change the world.

11

THE BUSINESS MODEL ACCORDING TO THE WOLF

The ideal business model is based on the naive customer who pays for products and services he doesn't need or rarely uses.

Business model? Ha! More like a model for how to screw people over and get paid for the privilege. I'm looking for customers who don't really know what they're doing. You know the type: people who are gullible enough to go for our substandard products. If they don't read the fine print, it's not my problem. I'm just in it for the money – and I'll take all I can get. It's all legal, so why should I worry? And if it's in that grey area on the edge, it wouldn't bother me a bit. If I don't do it, my competitors will, so why shouldn't I?

The Business Model According to the Dog

The ideal business model is based on how effectively you contribute to achieving your customers' goals.

Business models are more like value models. If I can work with my customer to evaluate whether the results are really worth it for them, I'll be creating a healthy business that everyone benefits from. Of course I'm making money, but I'm actually earning it! In a balanced value model, I'm giving my customers something that benefits them – and as the person delivering the value, I'm getting enough in return that I can take those profits and find ways to benefit them even more. Everyone wins! This positive spiral also makes me more successful, because empowered customers become active ambassadors who share my values and connect me to others who embrace the same philosophy.

The Sales Mantra According to the Wolf

The customer is your enemy.

How can I maximize how much money I make off my customers? How do I make sure that customers buy as many of my products as possible? How can I beat the competition? How can I find people who want to buy from me right this instant? How do I find customers who will buy my products? What killer arguments can I use to overcome any customer's objections and persuade them to buy? How can I overwhelm people so they can't say no to me anymore? Customers are never open; customers wiggle and pivot and never tell me the truth. Customers always want to get as much as they can for as little as possible; they want to suck me dry. How can I outsmart my customers? How can I get ahead, and how can I get rich? How do I screw everyone over?

The Sales Mantra According to the Dog

The customer is your friend.

Which of my customers' problems can I solve for them? What keeps my customers awake at night? How can my products help improve their lives? How can I make a difference for them? How can I show them that they can trust me? How can I let them see for themselves that who I am, what I offer, and the way I approach things will genuinely improve their situation? I want to be proud of my work. I want to be open and honest, and stand by what I say. I always want to be able to keep my promises. I really want to earn the money that I get for the work I do. Customers are my friends. Customers are people like you and me. Customers are open and share what they really think and feel and what they want. They deserve the best. They deserve my best. Customers should be totally wowed by the experience of working with me.

COMPETITION ACCORDING TO THE WOLF

You're competing for the customer's money,
and you deserve to get it all!

My competitors' products are worse than mine, just terrible. That's a given. I'm obviously the best, because I say so! I have a whole arsenal of killer one-liners carefully crafted to overwhelm any customer, dazzling them with promises and making any competitor look weak. The customer simply has to believe I'm the best. It's the cold, hard truth. He'd be crazy not to pick me. I make stuff up as I go along, gauging the customer's responses and tailoring my pitch to match. Anything goes, as long as the customer decides to buy our product. Our competitors are doing the same thing, so there's no need to hold back. If you can't stand the heat, get out of the kitchen. We're at war here! My words are weapons; my competitors are the enemy; the customer is the gleaming prize at the end.

COMPETITION ACCORDING TO THE DOG

The only true competitive edge here is fully maximizing potential value for the customer.

I prefer to focus on my own strengths, not my competitors' weaknesses. It's my job to really get to know what the customer wants, needs and hopes for. Once I know all that, I'm ideally positioned to see whether I can make life better for a potential customer. If I figure out how to maximize our contribution to improving my customer's situation, I won't have any competitors. Discussing the competition only distracts the customer from what really matters: the results they need. I'd rather work on building commitment from both sides to move things forward. My customer gets great value when they do business with me. The biggest threat I face is my own misjudgment: I need to be sure that I can serve this customer. If I can't, I shouldn't have invested my time in this project in the first place.

WHAT DOES THE MARKET REALLY WANT?

It's especially strong in product managers, startups, and the bright-eyed inventors of the world: they're proud of what their new product can do. The new feature, latest approach, unique combination... not sold anywhere else! It's great to see how proud people are of their latest business baby, with its boundless opportunities and billions of potential customers in the global marketplace. But if you ask them what problems the product will solve for their customer, they're often a loss for words. They're so focused on how shiny the product is that they've lost sight of why it was created in the first place. If you can offer what's relevant to the customer, you'll get their attention, but a keen feel for the market and a solid understanding of your customer's needs won't magically fall into your lap – especially not if you're all caught up in how glorious your new product is.

The point isn't to find a market for your products, but to develop products to meet market demand. In other words, you shouldn't be trying to force your product on the market. Instead, you should be trying to understand the market and meet the needs that aren't fully met yet.

This is incredibly important, because customers view a situation from their own perspective, their own context, and check whether products or services improve their situation for a reasonable price. If the sales professional, managing director, product developer, businessman, or bright-eyed inventor can respond to that need, they'll be able to explain how they can improve their customer's situation. That knowledge helps you understand your market better and adapt your products and services to the market even more effectively.

Wolves aren't all that interested in what the market wants; they just want to earn money and push their product. Dogs, on the other hand, understand the problems that need to be eliminated and can see when the product should be a priority for each customer – and can explain it clearly to the market. This approach moves sales out of the realm of blind product evangelization, a struggle for a few moments of the customers' attention, and transforms the sales process into a substantial, meaningful interaction that makes customers happy.

How Do We Start Selling?

Every market, product and customer is different. It's important to choose how you want to engage with your potential customers. The approach you take can have a major impact on your success and the nature of your business. Are your customers likely to complain about everything? Will they be prepared to pay more for your products? Will they be loyal, refer you to other customers, or not pay you at all if they can get away with it. Will they become your flagship customers, taking your company to the next level, or will they end up suing you and dragging your company through the mud? If there's one universal rule of sales, it's that you end up with the customers you deserve. Treat them like nothing more than a number, an insignificant detail, here today and gone tomorrow, and you'll find yourself being treated the same way. But rolling out the red carpet for every person who walks into your office or steps inside your digital world isn't all that practical either.

The trick is to find the ideal balance between personalizing your sales approach and automating processes to upscale your efforts. Wolves love to spam and automate everything, creating the illusion of personalization by replacing 'Dear Customer' with <first name> - but only fools respond to such obvious attempts to win their trust. Dogs, on the other hand, apply a methodical, account-based sales approach, building and nurturing a relationship and maximizing the value of each interaction. In areas where your customer doesn't require or desire personalization, let technology work for you. You'll be able to scale up and establish valuable relationships at the same time.

TARGET MARKET ACCORDING TO THE WOLF

Who cares where the money comes from,
as long as you get it?

I have a revenue problem, and customers are a potential solution to my problem. If people ask me, "who are your customers?" I always say, "anyone willing to buy from me". What a dumb question! I'm looking for buyers. Serious buyers. I generally just grab a list of leads, pick up the phone, and work my way through it, telling the same story to each one. I just keep calling until someone takes the bait. The fact that most of them aren't really interested or downright irritated that I'm calling them is just an occupational hazard. If I'm bugging them, that's just too bad; ignore the insults and strike when I find the right victim... I've just sharpened my teeth, so I'm all ready to go. Bring on the list!

TARGET MARKET ACCORDING TO THE DOG

*Which market niches need your capabilities
most urgently?*

The most important thing is to analyze and understand how customers are using my product or service and why it's worth something to them. What problems am I solving? Which of my customer's goals am I helping them achieve? Once I have a really solid understanding of how I can help, my next step is to analyze and define the ideal customer profile (ICP). In this process, I define the ICP as much as possible: buying personas, sectors, company size, culture, technology, location, growth phase, etc. I seek relevance and a high probability of a potential fit. Why would I try to serve people and companies that won't benefit as much from what I am capable of offering?

SALES STRATEGY ACCORDING TO THE WOLF

Strategy means cutting corners
to create the shortest route from A to Z.

Begin with the end in mind: the contract. I dive right in and take the direct approach, as direct as I can. Find contracts, find money, find customers, full stop. I find cunning ways to reach as many people as I can, as fast as possible. I fake a personalized approach, feigning interest in the other person so convincingly that most people don't even notice it. Have you ever tried writing your first email's subject line with the word 'RE:' at the beginning? Makes it look like you're replying to their message, so they're much more likely to open it! So funny; customers are so easy to fool. In any interaction, I go straight for the kill; that's my job. To be honest, I have one strategy and only one: focus on the deal and forget the rest. Sorry, gotta run; my fake LinkedIn profile is scheduled to give a fake webinar suggesting that I'm helping a customer implement our new solution – and it doesn't even exist yet! What a job, gotta love it! Never a dull moment.

SALES STRATEGY ACCORDING TO THE DOG

Strategy means adapting your approach
to each individual customer.

I know where my focus should be, so I approach a company that fits those parameters, with a specific purpose in mind. I figure out where people have a problem or seek to improve something that I think I can help them with. Not randomly, not by chance or coincidence, but targeted and personal. Not just by using their first name, obviously; that's too superficial. I start the dialogue by sharing my personal deeper understanding of the daily reality my customer lives in. Some people call it Account Based Selling. Essentially, it's about showing a genuine interest in making a positive impact for someone you haven't met yet. I invite you to have a meaningful dialogue. Are you ready?

MY VALUE PROPOSITION ACCORDING TO THE WOLF

The best USP automatically gets the deal.
And you're clearly the best!
(USP = Unique Selling Proposition)

Just look at my reflection in that mirror. Such a magnificent creature. There are so many wolves out there; I need to be bigger, better, stronger! I can't just be any old wolf. What makes me stand out? What's unique about me? Am I cheaper, do I deliver faster, are my products better, do I offer different features? What USPs can I blow out of proportion to build the foundation of my unique sales story? My customers need to know, because once they do, they'll buy from me. Yeah, baby! As soon as I contact a customer, I bombard them with all these benefits in such an incredibly appealing way that they're impressed beyond belief. They're thinking: this is the guy. I need to buy from him. Selling is so simple. Just listen to my story and you'll be sold.

MY VALUE PROPOSITION ACCORDING TO THE DOG

Find out your customer's UBRs,
so you know where you'll have the most impact.
(UBR = Unique Buying Reason)

Knowing my customer is the key to making a sale. Why should they buy what I'm offering? That's easy: because I'm sure it's what they need. Of course there's lots of alternative products out there, but my customer is my main focus. If I know their specific, unique reasons to buy, I can match them to my product. I won't know what's relevant to my customer until I know why they need it. If certain aspects of my product aren't relevant, what could they possibly be worth to the customer? I don't emphasize what makes my product different. It's not about being different; it's about making a difference.

PRICING

Everyone wants to make money – and making money isn't a bad thing. A healthy, profitable business model is a crucial success factor, and no commercial company can survive without one. However, the way you earn your money determines your customers' satisfaction, loyalty and ambassadorship – and how much they trust your company over time.

Cost or investment?

The price you charge for your products directly affects your bottom line – but pricing isn't about how much you can get away with. It's not easy to find an ideal balance between charging competitive prices, keeping customers satisfied, and maintaining your profit margins. Higher prices should represent greater value, and be communicated accordingly.

If a sales professional fails to convey the value their product could represent, customers can only differentiate by comparing the price. Sales professionals shouldn't be focused on what something costs, but on what it gives the customer. If it's just about the price, there's no reason not to shop for the cheapest option online, making the sales professional nothing more than an irrelevant middleman.

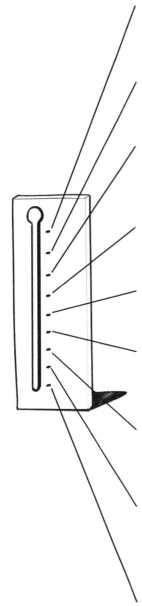

FRAUD
Sheer deception. It's all just a scam. There are no actual products, and customers get ripped off. Every cent you earn vanishes into your own pockets and customers are left with nothing.

THEFT
Even if you get away with it, your prices are so scandalously high that you'll eventually be dragged into court or demolished by a tell-all exposé on international TV.

OVERPRICED
You know you're asking too much for what you offer, and the sums of money you're raking in for your products are too good to be true. If this is standard policy at your company, you'll price yourself out of the market.

SMART DEAL
Good negotiators end up here. That includes dogs who've earned it by generating added value throughout the sales and negotiation process.

REASONABLE MARGIN
Most transactions end up here. Without exceptional sellers or buyers, this price point is often where the balance is achieved.

CHEAP
Great! You've got a new customer – but you haven't managed to prove to the customer that you're adding value, or you made too many concessions to close the deal, so it won't do you much good.

ROCK-BOTTOM DISCOUNT
At this point, you're more a bargain basement than a credible business offering value. If your profit margin is non-existent, your business model becomes unsustainable.

IRRESPONSIBLE
If your prices drop this low, you're hemorrhaging cash. Take a good, hard look in the mirror and ask yourself how you lost sight of your own interests. There's no way a customer could take you seriously as a potential business partner.

CHRISTMAS IN JUNE
You're basically just giving your products away. You're a philanthropist, not an entrepreneur. If you keep heading this direction, you're going to have to pay your customers for the privilege of handing your products over, and your business will crash and burn.

PRICING ACCORDING TO THE WOLF

The best price is obviously the highest price you can get away with.

Look, I know I get a lot of complaints – from colleagues and customers alike. So unfair! I make more deals than anyone. Seriously, no one else in our company is as good as I am. Some customers pay top dollar, even for parts that they could easily get for free. Don't tell anyone I said that, haha! But that's what makes me such a good sales professional: getting lots of money for doing as little as possible. Who wouldn't want that? I had to slash prices for other customers. We're too expensive, honestly. You know those buyers who do their research? So irritating when people explore the market ahead of time and know all about our competitors. But I want to nab those customers too! I get the deal done by making all sorts of empty promises. Why wait for internal approval? I'll weasel my way out of it later anyway. So what if the company doesn't end up earning anything on the account? I don't care; I'm still getting my bonus.

PRICING ACCORDING TO THE DOG

The best price is a price proportionate to the value being delivered.

I want to earn money. Not have it handed to me, not presented on a silver platter. No, I want to earn it. The price is proportionate to the value I deliver, and includes a healthy margin to allow us to constantly invest in my product – and my customer! There's some room to negotiate with customers on bigger projects, obviously, but we don't offer all that much wiggle room. Our prices don't go up or down that much; in both cases, I'm selling someone short – either myself or my customer. I rarely offer discounts. 9 times out of 10, they aren't even discussed. I appreciate customers who'd like to profit from the negotiations, make a good deal, but I'd rather charge my normal rates. Within that range, I discuss options with potential customers and see what they can accommodate. It's really simple: if they aren't willing to pay my price, then I didn't do a good enough job of proving the value of doing business with me and my organization.

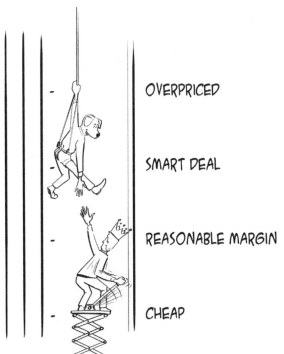

OVERPRICED

SMART DEAL

REASONABLE MARGIN

CHEAP

GETTING STARTED

TARGETS

A sales professional sees a target as both a blessing and a curse. Targets are often almost impossible to make, keeping you on your toes so you're motivated to move faster. You know that you're only as good as last quarter's performance, so it's the same hectic hustle every three months. The pressure is always on. And then there's the micromanager hovering over you with a spreadsheet, super-motivated to close the deal before the end of the month, quarter or year. That makes sense from the company's perspective, but it's completely irrelevant to the customer.

As a sales professional, it's important to make sure that you don't impose your company's internal deadlines on your customers in ways that slash your profit margins. The customer isn't remotely interested in some arbitrary reporting period that's coming to a close within your company. Your sales team will need customers next month too, so there's really no reason to sacrifice profits to temporarily boost those quarterly results. Plus, if customers know that salespeople are getting desperate to make end-of-year targets, they'll let you hit that desperation point over and over.

But what if sales are down and you're having trouble closing deals? Wolves respond by ramping up their activities to a frenzied pitch, running even faster in hopes of reaching even more customers and salvaging their year. That makes sense, because wolves are only interested in the results, not in how they got there. Dogs evaluate by taking a closer look at their chosen customers, the quality of their customer conversations, and how sales are made. Thorough problem analysis makes it possible to adapt your chosen sales strategy in order to improve results.

Planning the Year According to the Alpha Wolf

State how much money you want to make.

Sales planning starts with a sales target. I believe that targets enable us to aim higher and achieve great things. This is how much money I want to make. I just write that figure on the board and sell it to them. It doesn't really need to be that high, but setting inflated targets helps me keep my sales managers on their toes — and I get to keep the margin for myself. Besides, they'll do the same with their salespeople. The bonuses should keep them all hungry enough to ram the product down the customers' throats. A sale's a sale, right? I used to be exactly the same way; I used the same tactics. Thank goodness I no longer have to do that, because now I am the alpha wolf. And I genuinely don't care how, what or why, we just need to wring every last drop from the market. After all, those big fancy houses won't pay for themselves, will they?

Planning the Year According to the Top Dog

Measure additional potential customer value in the market

Sales planning starts with the customer. How satisfied are our customers? How many others could be ready to get that same great value from our product? How many potential customers are we talking about? Based on our customers' feedback, how can we support and serve our existing customers even better on their road to success? This is our growth potential. After that, I take a look at what I can realistically ask of my sales team and our organization so we can deliver on our promise to customers. As long as the customer experience is phenomenal, we will keep growing, which means we can keep investing in our products, people and the world around us.

Annual Speech According to the Wolf

Wolves are ready for action when
they're completely consumed by greed.

I have to keep my wolf pack lean and hungry, ready for anything. I need to keep them right on the edge. It's so simple: I generate competition and feed their greed. When they follow me, they can make tons of money. It's not for everyone, only the best of the best. Once I convince them they have to prove they're the best, I can make them frantic, make them do a-n-y-t-h-i-n-g to earn their bonuses. Obviously, I'll tell them it's so easy and that customers are just lining up to close a deal with us; they just don't know it yet. After all, we're the best! The very best. We are positively aglow with success. We dominate the scene. We are born winners. Anyone who can't make their target is a loser and deserves to be tossed out. Sure, not everybody is a born salesperson. You've either got what it takes, or you'll never learn. I can make as much money as I want here; it's ripe for the taking. Take a long look at my nice, fat bank account. Look at me; this is what success looks like!

ANNUAL SPEECH ACCORDING TO THE DOG

Dogs are ready for action when
they realize what they mean to customers.

We're not just here to sell something; we are on a mission. We have a unique and inspiring goal that we want to achieve together, making a major impact in the industry. We're doing exceptional things here, and we all have a chance to contribute. It is important for my people to hear from our customers how much they appreciate us, why they chose to work with us, and why we matter to them and the market. Customer excitement makes our dogs become even stronger ambassadors – and their enthusiasm will be transferred to new customers. Money is important, but it's a limited motivator in improving sales and generating sustainable relationships. We're not looking for the next quick deal, picking up insignificant little contracts that don't represent much. We're looking for customers that we can share our journey with.

THE SALES PROCESS ACCORDING TO THE WOLF

The selling phase tells you how close you are to your commission.

Sales process, blablabla, whatever. Just meet my customers, generate interest, send a proposal and rake those deals in. A real sales professional knows how to get the customer to sign as soon as possible. That's the point, right? Get that signature and move on. I just toss as many potentials into the funnel as possible. It's all about the numbers game. I send proposals as fast as I can to as many companies as possible, negotiate a bit, and the cat's in the bag! Of course our CRM system is supposed to make it all more official, but I've learned to manipulate it to my advantage. The beauty of it is, since I just chuck everything I do in there, it creates the illusion that I'm a star seller. That's how I get things done around here. Who cares that it's not as good as it looks? The fact that most of these deals fall through and the forecast is a joke couldn't possibly be my fault. We're just too expensive. Obviously, our product simply isn't good enough, or I would have sold even more. It's my manager's own fault for wanting me to put everything in the system. You get what you ask for! Now stop bugging me; I've got to go sell something to someone.

Selling Phase	Automatic crm %	Example with a negative customer	Actual %
Cold call	5%	Maximum indifference	0%
First meeting	10%	Didn't really want the appointment	0%
Second meeting	15%	He said he was in the neighborhood	0%
Presentation	20%	Annoying and tiresome; the guy insisted on presenting	0%
Proposal	25% (only 4 bidders)	Didn't take up our time, but we did get pricing information	0%
Negotiation	75%	He offered the lowest price if we decided fast. We could, just not with him. We aren't stupid!	0%
Deal / no deal	100%	That's a definite no	0%

THE SALES PROCESS ACCORDING TO THE DOG

The buying phase shows where the customer is in his buying journey.

I'm more interested in where the customer's at in their buying journey than my own sales process. If I know how far along the customer is, I can choose the best strategy for connecting with my customer and maximizing my impact in a very positive way. For instance, I want to find out why my customers are interested, what they really need, what it takes for them to reach that decision within their company, and their most ideal time to implement a new solution. They are following their own process; if I'm familiar with the sequence and pace, I can anticipate their next steps and guide them through it. I mainly use my CRM system to track how far along my customers are, so I always know how and when to strike a chord with my customers. In the end, I'll secure a successful outcome for them and therefore myself.

Customer's buying phase	manual % input by sales person	Situation at the customer	Actual %
Customer shares relevant information	5%	Was a good conversation, wants to see the salesperson again	5%
Customer want to change status quo	10%	Conclusion: change is necessary	10%
Customer seeks solution	15%	Decided to determine requirements	15%
Customer prefers your type of solution	20%	Decided to replace equipment instead of repair	20%
Customer learns about your offer	25%	Looked good and seemed like a robust solution	25%
Customer sees a good match	30%	We noticed their solution fits and they have the right expertise	30%
Customer validates investment	50%	Calculated the new system will save us costs	50%
Customer sets buying date	60%	We want to implement before the 3rd quarter	60%
Customer accepts conditions	75%	Service conditions need to be adapted to our needs; we require weekend hours	75%
Decision yes/no	100%	Both boards sign together to increase mutual commitment	100%

System Overload

Market research reveals that we encounter over 13,000 marketing messages on an average day. We're constantly bombarded with brands, products and information, whether we want to see it or not: everywhere we go, at home, in the office or on the streets, on television, radio, phone, billboards, flyers, restaurant screens: on and on and on.

This constant onslaught of unsolicited information continues at work. Once we reach the office, we receive countless emails and phone calls. Our mental hard drives are overflowing with incredible amounts of data. And that's not even considering our busy personal lives! Hobbies, friends, family, sports, travel: our calendars are packed. Our potential buyers have zero time and energy to familiarize themselves with all the companies, products and suppliers out there. In fact, if they really took their time to understand all the options at their disposal, they'd be the worst managers ever, because they'd have no time to do anything else! Customers are going crazy trying to keep up with the flood of information.

This presents a major challenge for sales professionals. If you want to sell your product or service, you need to get the buyer's attention – but you don't want to be that guy who's bugging them at the office, keeping them from getting their real work done. Companies who aren't ready to identify their needs, and are therefore not looking for a solution right now, aren't going to be your buyers – not yet, anyway. So now what? To get their attention, don't try to sell yet. Instead, a marketer or sales professional can share relevant, interesting information and expertise to the potential buyer. Potential buyers can take what they've picked up and immediately apply it within their company. This form of content marketing can be very effective and is a great initial introduction. And just so we're clear, for the wolves out there: content marketing is not the same as product information.

If a company realizes they need something, digital sources like Google and LinkedIn are considered ideal ways to find relevant information and possible solutions. When a potential buyer contacts a supplier at this stage, it is important that the sales professional brings more to the table than product or pricing information. If that's all they're contributing, the customer could just as easily consult the company website instead. And it's too early to try to close a deal at this stage; attempts to speed up the process won't add any value to potential buyers. Pushing the issue will only create resistance that the sales person has to break down again in order to move forward.

Sometimes sales professionals succumb to a pervasive syndrome, assuming that the customer needs to know everything about the company as soon as possible. When that happens, it's tempting to cram all the available information down a potential buyer's throat. That's counterproductive! The secret lies in only providing relevant information and constantly connecting it to the customer's context. That approach is only effective when it's based on a solid understanding of the industry and current trends, as well as the customer's business processes. When you're a valued partner who maintains an equal dialogue with a potential customer, you can start asking the right questions and building value from the outset. Once you've established that rapport, the customer won't hesitate to make time for you and learn about their new business opportunity.

MARKETING ACCORDING TO THE WOLF

There's no such thing as bad publicity; just get your name out there.

Everybody should know about us. Whether my customers are thrilled with my involvement or not, our name should be everywhere - commercials, banners, emails — so no one overlooks our market presence. Who cares what they're saying, as long as they're talking about us. In fact, customer complaints are free publicity; after all, they're getting our brand out there! Whatever it takes, as long as everyone recognizes our name. Haven't researchers already proven that people prefer to do business with brands they recognize? There you go! Customers are idiots anyway; they'll spontaneously buy our products because they recognize our name. The true essence of marketing is name recognition and conversion. Regardless of what we do, there are a thousand ways for customers to book a meeting, schedule a demo, or simply give us fistfuls of cash. Once I actually meet the customer, I'll put a nice spin on all the negativity. I'll just tell them about how fantastic our products are and they'll swallow it hook, line and sinker. They'll buy any bullshit story I feed them! God, I love my job!

MARKETING ACCORDING TO THE DOG

The best publicity is customers raving about how great you are.

Don't tell people you're funny; just tell a joke and let your audience nudge each other and laugh together. Personal reviews are what really convince customers – so the best publicity is seriously satisfied customers who promote my product without prompting. Not because they are being rewarded, but because they're such huge fans that they want to tell the whole world about their great experience. Sure, publicity and promotion are important: if no one knows I even exist, they're unlikely to buy my products. When we communicate in the marketplace, our audience should discover something useful from what we're saying, no matter how small. We are familiar with their problems and the challenges they face, and we know how our product will help them overcome those issues and move forward. That's what we want to convey: our in-depth expertise and specific knowledge.

ADVERTISING ACCORDING TO THE WOLF

Advertising is force-feeding your brand into the market.

How can potential customers buy from me if they don't know me, or can't find me? Our name has to be a household byword, universally present wherever customers look; that celebrity status gives me a nice opening so I can jump right in and talk about where we excel. All our ads, banners, and marketing materials should be showcasing what makes us #1. We should be shouting that we're the greatest, cheapest, fastest, guaranteed best quality, whatever – it doesn't have to be true, as long as it sounds good. Tack on a nondescript slogan that sounds catchy without really saying anything, and we're all set to outshine the competition. Never overestimate customers. They're so gullible, they'll believe anything I promise. It's not like they really know the difference anyway! If I'm loud and proud, I'll convince them, even if it's all a sham. That's sales!

ADVERTISING ACCORDING TO THE DOG

Advertising is giving a taste at what you can deliver.

Sure, I could sit here and list all the reasons why we're fantastic... but we've seen that our customers have grown numb to the hyperbole. We're all surrounded by a flood of short, superficial messages; why bother adding to that? I believe in relevant, content-rich information that encourages engagement and dialogue. Every time we interact with our customers, we aim to achieve a positive impact. Customers should be able to use what we're saying. That's why we rely on content marketing: not explaining the product itself, but talking about why it's important, sharing how it has helped other people, letting people know what motivated our customers to pick us. I mean seriously, isn't it fantastic when customers can share experiences and help each other become even more successful? And this approach helps me connect with the right type of customers — because that's the best way to achieve success for me and for my customers.

SOCIAL MEDIA IN SALES ACCORDING TO THE WOLF

*Social media is about maintaining a convincing
façade despite all the negativity.*

Sales professionals should stay off social media. It's just a cesspool of complaints; everyone's so negative! People complain about shoddy service or whine that a product wasn't delivered exactly as expected. It's not a perfect world; get over it! There's plenty more fish in the sea, so who cares if a couple customers aren't satisfied? I don't take it personally, though, since they're criticizing the company and not me. It's not like I do anything online under my own name. The less people know about me, the better, so I can pretend to be anything I want when I'm pitching a sale. Fair enough, sometimes I get caught out, but it's not the end of the world – as long as I get that signature at the bottom of the contract most of the time. The marketing team is responsible for making us look good; they should be writing fake reviews themselves, or hiring low-wage workers to post positive comments. I'm just waiting to rake in those commissions and bonuses. Once I've collected enough cash, I'm off to the Bahamas! See ya...

SOCIAL MEDIA IN SALES ACCORDING TO THE DOG

Social media is about bringing your network and customers together to inspire the digital world.

I love to spend time on social media! I'm delighted to have a direct way to share interesting, relevant information – especially about what I'm working on. I love finding new opportunities to inspire the people around me. It's so beautiful to see customers sharing their positive experiences about working with me and my company, recommending me to their entire network. Fair, honest, sincere reviews, written, posted and shared online by my own customers! Potential customers can see first-hand, unmanipulated proof that I truly want my product to achieve a positive change for my customers. Time is always on my side, because I know that every customer I serve will affirm my reputation. The community will only grow bigger and bigger, as I work with the right customers and exceed their expectation time and time again. My approach is transparent for all to see, because I am proud of the way I do business. My customers handle my social media presence on my behalf, out of sheer gratitude. That's the best possible proof that I'm doing it right – and that's exactly why others believe all this positive coverage on social media. It's authentic!

Developing New Business

Leads to Chase

Let's disregard the debate about whether cold calls are effective. It's pretty simple: badly executed cold calling never works and will only end up giving you a bad market rep. At its worst, bad cold calling turns into anti-marketing. But what's the alternative? If you never pick up the phone and proactively contact potential customers, that can't be good for business either. Phone calls are still a good way to get in touch with lots of fantastic people within a short time frame. If you do pick up the phone and reach out, then at least start out with a hook, an opener that launches a meaningful dialogue. If your hook is relevant, topical and interesting, there's a better chance that your added value will be obvious during the phone call. Wolves are lazy and don't bother to figure out if they're calling the right person, but dogs do their research and know what they're getting into, so their hook is right on target and they're no longer calling cold.

Here's a few hooks you could consider using, in combination or individually:

- Refer to a specific project that's high on your prospect's agenda, and mention how your product or service could make a positive contribution. You could note that you learned about the project through your own research, your company's annual report or your extended business network.
- Mention a success story involving a reference customer that has key characteristics in common with the company you're calling.
- Mention similar customers with the same title (such as IT Director or Logistics Manager) who had a specific problem that you helped them resolve, explaining how that situation correlates to the company you're contacting.
- Refer to a relevant quote from an article, LinkedIn post, tweet, or other media statement from the company you're contacting, preferably from the person you have on the phone; follow with a logical segue to your own product or service.
- Approach a potential buyer based on a recommendation from a mutual business acquaintance, customer or colleague; let them know you're contacting them because someone they already know and trust told you they'd be interested.

The key to success is preparation and routine. Cold calling a complete stranger based on meaningless references to generic statements on their website is superficial and pointless. The suggestion that you could have anything to offer on that basis actually makes you sound calculating at best and incompetent at worst. However, if you find the right combination of hooks and do your prep, your phone call will feel logical and relevant. If you manage to master this technique and make it second nature, no phone call will feel awkward – not to you and not to your potential customer.

LEADS TO DEVELOP

There's nothing a sales professional likes better than a juicy lead handed to them on a silver platter. Someone contacts you and asks you to call or email them. Hurray! But don't get complacent; there are wolves and dogs in many professions, and not every buyer has good intentions. Some ostensible buyers might just be trying to find out your prices – for benchmarking purposes, to undercut you in the market, or to support their negotiations with some other provider. Sales professionals run a simple risk here: spending time on people who aren't actually interested. The hours you spend chasing down a lead that turns out not to be serious represent wasted time that you'll never get back. Focus your time and energy on viable leads by identifying whether you're dealing with a wolf or a dog.

Ask the right questions:
- How long has the company been searching for this product or service?
- Which other suppliers has the company already contacted?
- Why is the company reaching out to you?
- What added value is the company hoping to find that has been missing from other suppliers' proposals?
- What is the company planning to do with the offer?
- What does the company hope to achieve from the purchase?
- Besides the price, what else do they consider important?

PITCH ACCORDING TO THE WOLF

Your pitch is the greatest; never change a thing!
You're just that awesome.

Of course I never call myself a wolf! Jack sounds more legit, so I'll just use that name instead. It's all about creating the impression that people can trust me. People respect strength and confidence, so when I run into a potential customer, I make myself look powerful and start pitching. I tell everybody in the strongest possible terms who we are and why we are so great. I throw in high numbers to impress others. Are they accurate? Nah, why bother? It's fine to inflate the figures; that is the essence of selling. I emphasize that only losers don't choose to buy from us, because all the best people are with us. Now the customer feels peer pressure; psychological pressure is a convenient way to boost interest. Who wouldn't want to do business with a successful company? I should be the key player that no one can ignore.

THE PITCH ACCORDING TO THE DOG

Your pitch should be different every single time:
level with the customer.

I believe we should be proud of the value we represent for our customers and share that with the world. But there's another dimension to that. Every time I present a pitch, I want to make a genuine connection with the person I'm talking to. Just talking about myself or our product without explaining the relevance is just so much hot air. I always ask great questions to ensure my words carry meaning and weight. When I ask questions, I can quickly identify who I'm talking to and respond authentically to my audience. How I have helped other people and companies, and why they appreciated the collaboration: these relevant details are always part of my pitch. The pitch is never fabricated from thin air; I build it in conjunction with the customer. The goal is to trigger interest and discover common ground to pursue the dialogue. I love pitching, since it allows me to discover new opportunities to make a difference.

Gatekeepers according to the wolf

The secretary is an annoying, pointless intermediary who's in the way.

All right, fine, actually lying is wrong, but a little white lie? Come on, don't take it too seriously! ;-) I twist and turn things here and there, make it sound a little better by leaving a couple details out, pretend a bit. Who cares, as long as it works? My most important objective? To get through to the decision maker. When I envision a secretary or assistant picking up the phone, I see a big, burly bouncer in front of me, a hulking linebacker blocking my way to the big boss. This gatekeeper is a mere insect, far beneath me; half-brained and incompetent, they're certainly not someone I'd consider an equal dialogue partner. I've got my usual high-powered one-liners all ready to go, so I'll sound catchy and convincing regardless of who I'm talking to. Take it or leave it; plenty more fish in the sea if this one's not biting. I'm poised to bait the hook with convenient exaggerations or shrewd tactics; I'll try intimidating bluff if necessary. All I'm looking for is one moment of weakness. I find my opening and I'm in. I'm not just any old wolf... Yee-haw!

GATEKEEPERS ACCORDING TO THE DOG

The secretary is perfectly positioned to help access the right people.

I believe in real, authentic contact with every person I encounter – and I believe we catch more flies with honey than with vinegar. There's a decent chance that I'll be talking to this secretary on a regular basis, especially if I end up in a commercial venture with the boss. The secretaries I speak are often more than prepared to help me connect – not only with the major decision-maker, but also other relevant key influencers in a possible project. I come prepared, so I have a legitimate reason to reach out that particular company, department and person. By contributing genuine interest and potential opportunities, I bring something to the table instead of trying to exploit the situation. My transparent approach creates a context in which the content of what I'm offering is just as important as who I am. Sure, it doesn't always succeed; secretaries have encountered so many wolves in their line of work! Once bitten, twice shy, so it's vital for this person to realize that I'm nothing like that. The more authentic and real I am, the more likely I am to make a difference and establish rapport.

Booking sales meetings according to the wolf

Always go for the meeting. Always.

Once I've made the pitch, the customer responds. He'll generally turn me down, but that's part of the game. I need to keep the conversation going just long enough to have time to sell the appointment again. Not too long, though, because I don't want the customer to have time to come up with objections. I have to beat the customer to it, overpower him by using effective rebuttals before he can escape my grasp. If he still resists, I have to come up with another way to outwit him – for example by saying I'm already in the neighborhood anyway, or I only need 20 minutes. Sure, both of these are stretching the truth, but who cares? The more tricks I have up my sleeve, the better. All I need is a chance to tell my story. I won't know whether it's worth my time or not until I give it a shot, so I just make an appointment, suit up, and head out to our next customer. Let's go get 'em!

BOOKING SALES MEETINGS ACCORDING TO THE DOG

If both parties see an opportunity, meeting is the logical next step.

Once I've made the pitch, it's crucial for me to demonstrate my expertise and added value by asking the right questions. The goal here isn't just to trigger the customer, but to work together to discover mutual opportunities. If that happens, I'll be able to make an appointment because the customer has decided he'd like to meet, which sets the stage for success. I want to ensure that the customer considers the appointment a priority and reserves enough time for it. Other sales professionals often complain about customers who cancel appointments, postpone them indefinitely, or don't even bother to show up. I rarely have that problem. My time is too important to waste – and so is my customer's! Let's make it count.

FACE-TO-FACE

The first sales meeting is a defining moment in the sales process, crucial to ensuring your customer commits. A great first meeting gets you off to a perfect start, while a bad first impression can kill an opportunity before it even gets off the ground. First impressions are everything. Not just when you walk in and shake hands, but even more so when the customer contemplates who you are and what you're offering once you leave the room. The customer will be asking himself, 'Is this the type of person I'd be willing to buy from, regardless of product or value?' He'll wonder: "If I do business with this sales professional, what can I expect, will I benefit from the process, and would I enjoy working with this person?'

Trust can only be given freely; it can't be forced

It's impossible to cover everything in that first meeting, so the sales professional and the customer determine the priorities mutually. No two sales meetings are the same, because that first encounter involves widely diverse individuals in interaction – and every sales professional has their own preferred way to handle a sales meeting. So what would be the prime parameters for an ideal sales meeting?

Yes please!	Let's not
Great introduction, with sufficient time to get to know each other	Rant about yourself and how great you are
Comprehensive analysis of the customer's situation	Immediately talk about your own products
Clear, concise identification of the problems you could potentially solve for the customer	Jump quickly from customer problems to your solution, instead of analyzing their situation first
Summary of possible benefits for the customer, framed in a way that leads them to the conclusion instead of announcing it	List customer benefits yourself, instead of letting the customer discover the benefits through your story
Define the follow-up steps that are required to reach a mutual decision.	Let the meeting end with a single next step, without co-creating any type of plan with the customer

Earning the Right to Ask High-Impact Questions

Active listening is more important than smooth-talking or spin. However, you can subtly influence what the customer tells you. If you don't broach the right subjects and ask the right questions, the customer won't offer you the right information, so you'll end up hearing superficial or irrelevant details. If you do manage to ask the right questions, you might hear objectives, motives, challenges, issues, projects, strategic choices, priorities, relationships, interests, interdepartmental interactions, personal ambitions, etc. All this information could offer crucial opportunities to show potential added value. However, not all customers are prepared to open up and share what's happening behind the scenes at their company.

However, if you confront a prospective customer with detailed questions too soon or too blatantly, you're sure to encounter resistance – and that'll keep you from getting the answers you need. How do you earn the right to ask these types of questions without making the customer feel like you're taking advantage of them?

Your customer is more likely to open up if you're able to:
- Demonstrate that his best interests are the main priority of the meeting;
- Show how you've helped similar companies;
- Share your knowledge of the customer's company based on your background research;
- Let him know you have a structured process, know where you're headed, and know which information you'll need to identify the specific benefits for this customer;
- Start out with 'safe', general questions so you can gather relevant data and start aligning your products or services to the customer's company.

THE SALES MEETING ACCORDING TO THE WOLF

It's all about making money,
so focus on what the customer is worth to you.

A good sales professional has a keen eye for doing business. That's why I mainly focus on the authority to make a decision, the available budget, when they want to do business, and why they would opt for us. Those aspects are key; the rest is secondary. In order to get there, I usually start off with a compliment on how lovely the office is, a remark about artwork, whatever it takes to set a positive tone. I check how the customer responds, then mirror whatever he does. Then I establish a pattern of positive reinforcement: it's time to get the customer used to saying YES. I start asking simple questions that he'll affirm. It's a tried-and-tested technique that makes it more likely he'll say YES when it's time to close the deal. Making the sale is a piece of cake, really. Once the customer's agreeing with me, I switch to decision-making, budget, which product and when: exactly what I need to know to make it happen. And of course I mention that our company's honest, customer-driven and so on – all those reassuring words that customers want to hear. That's the best approach. Believe me, I know!

THE SALES MEETING ACCORDING TO THE DOG

It's all about improvement,
so the main priority is identifying where you can contribute.

I'm like a doctor: diagnose first, treat second. I need to analyze the situation before prescribing the best medicine! Sure, we first need to figure out if we have good chemistry, do a bit of chit-chat to establish a positive atmosphere, and make sure we're introduced properly; that's all part of my profession. But once we've gotten the preliminaries out of the way, I'm mainly interested in the company and the person I'm talking to. I analyze the situation and its specific challenges, I make that first, quick judgment call to gauge whether my product suits the customer's problems and whether a transaction would be valuable. I don't tell the customer that we're customer-driven or honest, I show it! I want to ensure that the customer understands that our potential added value for their company is my top priority here. When that happens, customers always open up to me and are more than happy to entrust me with their business-critical information, so I can serve them even better. We become partners working towards a common goal: to benefit the customer. Once all the relevant information is on the table, we can sit down and incorporate it into a co-created strategy for the most appropriate next steps.

... SO WE TRIED THAT, BUT IT DIDN'T REALLY WORK OUT. WE CONCLUDED THAT WE NEEDED TO EXPLORE ALTERNATIVE APPROACHES, SUCH AS ...

SALES PRESENTATIONS ACCORDING TO THE WOLF

Convince the customer that your story is the best;
that's the only way to make the sale.

This is the Hallelujah! moment. It's my time to shine. I'm going to take charge and tell the customer what's what, leaving him no alternative: we're his only logical choice! I won't let the customer talk much during the presentation; that only distracts from my main message. I build up the story properly, showing how great our product is and how it can guarantee success based on our other customers. I also make good use of my voice and presence, so their attention will not slip for a single second. They're not allowed to miss any details of my presentation; otherwise they might not buy anything! At the perfect point in my story, I'll discuss budget again and ask to close the deal. That's how I find out who is making the real decisions. I never leave without making sure I have their full commitment. Just try and say no to me. I AM THE WOLF!!!!

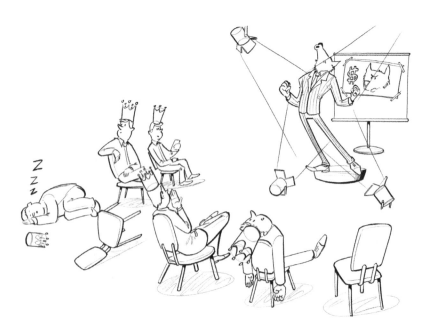

SALES PRESENTATIONS ACCORDING TO THE DOG

Show the customer where your solution meet his needs,
and he'll be ready to consider buying.

My story isn't the focus here. The presentation is always about the customer's story. The presentation and our information are only used to deepen our interaction with the customer. In the presentation, I like to discuss my perspective on the company's key objectives and the customer's main problem so I'm sure everyone is on the same page. After that, I want to confirm what the customer's main goals are and what kind of impact they want to see once the issue is resolved, so we can talk about how our products and solutions can help them achieve that result. My very favorite moment is when I get to brainstorm with the customer on the best way to implement our product in their context. I know the customer is ready to move forward if he can convince me why our solution is best for him. If the customer is truly convinced, that confidence in our solution will maximize the chances of another resounding success. The journey is just as important as the destination.

PROVIDING PROOF ACCORDING TO THE WOLF

The customer should be convinced you are the best.

Look, customers are always hesitant, but their doubts are just part of the deal. I have a one-page document stating that we're #1 across the board, and I bring it with me everywhere. I use carefully crafted words and phrases to describe our long track record in business, our vast experience, our state-of-the-art products... And of course I mention maximum customer satisfaction, positive feedback, five-star ratings from independent agencies. No need to mention our weaknesses, right? The point is to showcase our strengths. If potential customers bring up a weak point, I ignore it or laugh it off as an irrelevant side note. Oh, and those customer reviews? I wrote them myself! Or had our marketing team make them up for me. And that independent agency? We invented it! The whole thing's a farce, haha! Gotta love it. Selling is all about perceptions, so I make sure I manipulate them in my favor.

PROVIDING PROOF ACCORDING TO THE DOG

It's time to validate that the customer will benefit.

Of course I believe in my product, but I find it just as important to be sure that the product will make a solid contribution to my customer's specific situation. Ideally, we'll sit down together and take an objective look at whether it's the right solution for them. I'm always looking for ways to do a test, on-site demo, quick scan, pilot project or trial period, if that's what it takes for both of us to be 100% sure we should move forward to full implementation or purchase. I often run the numbers with potential customers, helping them calculate savings and gains in various scenarios. Those cold, hard figures make it easier for the customer to verify that the product will work and validate his investment. I see it as my job to empower my customer to communicate the value of my products, acting as an effective brand ambassador within his own company. If the proof of the pudding is in the eating, it's time to start serving!

Homework

Once the sales professional has conducted a thorough analysis of the customer's situation, it's time to collate all that information into a proposal that resonates with the customer. The sales professional will have to structure the background details and analysis results so they clearly connect to the customer's situation, leading to a customer-driven proposal. Now the customer can see how well the sales professional has actually understood what he needs and why – and confirm that you're taking his situation seriously.

The proposal should clarify why you're suggesting specific products or solutions. Your in-depth business acumen, relevance, meticulous approach and added value will have a significant impact on the customer's willingness to buy. If your proposal is limited to an overview of products and prices, the customer is left to guess why it's worth his time and money. Make sure you're linking your products to the customer's context, so you minimize the risk that the customer will misinterpret your proposal or overlook key areas where you're offering added value.

Timing is crucial. Don't present your proposal before you're ready! Once you share your proposal with your customer, you're not just providing product and pricing information; you're also revealing who you are. At that point, you're putting all your metaphorical cards on the table. If your proposal is incomplete or unclear, based on incorrect assumptions, sent too soon, or addressed to the wrong people, or does not meet expectations, you'll end up being ignored; the customer will simply stop returning your calls. If that happens, your potential customer will write you off entirely, dismissing you as an amateur rather than embracing you as a competent sales professional and equal business partner.

Is your customer a complete novice?

Sales professionals often have to deal with customers who have little to no knowledge or experience in your field, and may never have heard of the product or service you're selling. Some cutting-edge sectors are so new that almost no one has any prior experience with your products, and are therefore incapable of accurately assessing quality or relevance, let alone deciding whether to buy. This is a unique opportunity for sales professionals!

You are now ideally positioned to share your expert knowledge, facilitate your customer's learning experience, add value, and make a real difference. A wolf might smell easy prey and take advantage, driving prices up and saddling customers with unnecessary products and services. We've all heard the B2C horror stories about car mechanics, plumbing emergencies, building contractors, mortgage suppliers, or door-to-door solar panel salesmen... In a mature, competitive, transparent market, buyers have more alternatives and can make better choices on their own. In emergent markets involving less transparency, you'll see a major contrast between wolves and dogs. Here's a chance for you to make a real contribution!

How do you handle less well-informed customers?

Wolf	Dog
Abuses lack of knowledge	Shares expertise and information
Keeps the customer weak	Empowers the customer
Maintains customer naivety	Makes customer aware
Seeks to maximize complexity	Seeks simplicity
Creates confusion	Creates clarity
Reinforces dependency	Encourages autonomy

QUALIFICATION* ACCORDING TO THE WOLF

Seize each and every sales opportunity; try anything, anytime!

Yeah, sure, I've heard of qualification. But honestly, I think I just need to be so incredibly effective in any situation that I can take a shot at any sales opportunity. Chance to meet? Let's do it! Opportunity to send a proposal? Go for it! Option to present? Never say no! I am the quintessential optimist and I'm convinced I can persuade anyone to buy from me. I love putting myself out there, visiting companies, persuading people to do business with me. I'm a real people person. Well... that's the impression I'm trying to make, anyway! In actual fact, I just love manipulating people. The whole sales charade is one big numbers game. The more customers I talk to, the more I sell. It doesn't matter how small the odds are, I have to jump in and respond ASAP, faster than anyone else – and no one's faster than me! I'm the supreme king of copy/paste replies around here.

*Qualification = the art of assessing how attractive a sales opportunity could be.

QUALIFICATION ACCORDING TO THE DOG

Spend time on opportunities that you believe in, with good reason.

Knowing why I'm doing what I do is vitally important! Before I head out to meet a customer or send an initial proposal, I always analyze why I'm pursuing this. I take a good, hard look at whether the time I'm putting into it is proportionate to the possible value I might offer the customer, and whether I'm likely to succeed. I need to justify to myself why I am spending my time on this specific customer. I don't do anything halfway; if I'm going to spend time on something, I take it seriously and make sure I add value. If a company is too small for my solution to work well for them, if the customer is unlikely to take my proposal or product seriously, if the scope of what I'm offering is too big for their needs, or if we're simply not a good match, then I should move on. My time is valuable, and so is theirs; I want to focus on projects where I can make a real difference. Customers sometimes don't fully comprehend the risks of moving too quickly. It is my job to decide what to spend time on. I can achieve a lot for my customers, but only if we both believe in what we're doing.

WHAT TO OFFER ACCORDING TO THE WOLF

What will maximize revenues and profit margins?

Obviously, I've assessed what I think this customer would realistically want to spend – but I'm in this for the money, so I add just enough to pad my margins. Why would I hold back if I can get even more out of him? The way I see it, the customer's money is basically my money. I always recommend the most expensive products I can offer, the ones that earn me the best commission. Then all I need to do is convince everyone those products are perfect! And of course I never just show customers exactly what they're asking for. No, cross-selling is where it's at: additional features, extra accessories, fancy add-ons, whatever I can tack on the end where he's least likely to notice how much it's adding up. Customers are always so stupid! All right, sure, I get it: it's not like the customer actually benefits from all these extras, but who cares? That's not my fault; he should have done his homework ahead of time and figured out what he actually needed. I'm not here to advise him on his purchases; I'm here to sell!

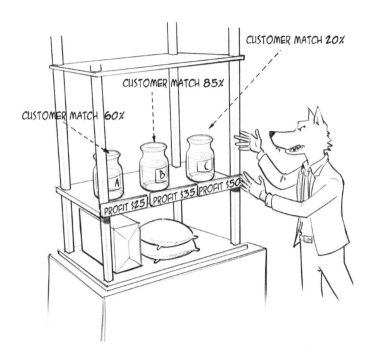

WHAT TO OFFER ACCORDING TO THE DOG

What will maximize customer value and create customer loyalty?

I always try to find the best possible solution to my customer's problem, looking at the situation from the customer's perspective to maximize effective impact. I look at our products, possible adaptations or minor adjustments: whatever I can find to achieve optimum gains for my customer. Value first, then price. Once the customer approves the proposal, I can rest assured he's definitely getting the best possible solution; that's my main priority. That's why I keep my proposals streamlined, limiting the content to exactly what we discussed and only addressing the most important problems. If I offer extra options or accessories, or suggest related products, it will only distract from achieving our mutual objective. I am 100% sure that my proposal is solid, or I wouldn't have made it in the first place.

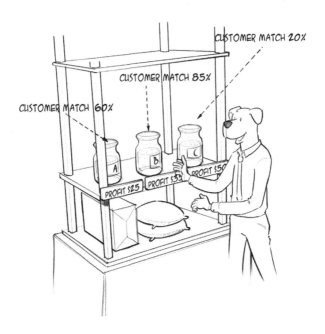

THE PROPOSAL ACCORDING TO THE WOLF

Use cookie-cutter proposals for pricing and products; it's up to the customer to figure out what he actually needs.

Those proposals have to get out there as fast as possible. Like I said, it's a numbers game. The more I send out, the better. Proposals have to look sleek, printed in color on quality paper. They should be easy to read, too. Standard texts, carefully crafted by our marketing team, based on a beautifully structured template. Our proposals have it all: a boilerplate stating who we are, our company's history and values, and our complete line of products with all their features and benefits. There's only one flaw in this system: going through and replacing the customer's name! Sometimes I forget and some other poor schmuck's name is still on the proposal. Ah well, doesn't matter; sloppy mistakes like that just give me another reason to contact them! Oh, and I firmly believe in giving customers options, even if there isn't really much difference; they love feeling like they're making a smart choice! Pro tip: mostly they just go for the one in the middle, like ordering medium fries at McDonalds. Pop psychology at its finest!

PROPOSALS SHOULD BE **90%** COPY/PASTE. LOL, LOOK AT THAT LOSER OVER THERE, WORKING HIS BUTT OFF TO CUSTOMIZE IT EVERY TIME!

The Proposal According to the Dog

The proposal is a summary of all the conversations, stating what the customer can expect in terms of deliverables, pricing and ROI.

The beauty of drafting a proposal is that I get to show the customer that I really heard what he was saying and understand what's relevant. I include a summary of our conversations, phrased in such a way that the proposal can be shared and understood by different departments and decision-makers throughout the company. It's essential for the customer to comprehend the logic behind what I'm offering, so he has confidence in the core principles in the proposal. If there's an additional product I was planning to demonstrate during the sales meeting and forgot to mention, I won't add it to the proposal. This isn't the right place to make up for my own mistakes; that can be addressed later on in our working relationship. I keep my proposal to what's relevant to the customer; anything else just distracts from the main objective.

Overcoming Resistance

Originally, potential customers had limited access to alternatives, so sales professionals were all-powerful. We had something important to offer that they couldn't get anywhere else: our products! We used that power to pressure customers, pestering them at unexpected moments and using clever tricks to grab attention and talk about our products. Based on that approach, you'd just keep stalking your customer until they had a moment of weakness and agreed to meet with you. Once you got that meeting, you could just go through the motions, well-prepared to refute any objections and willing to do or say anything to get your customer to sign. Once you forced that YES, you'd move on to the next easy mark. Since anyone could be a customer, sales professionals were trained to ignore every objection and push forward. Sales competence was measured purely in terms of how many NOs could be converted into a YES. These 'push skills' became the definition of great salesmanship.

The world is changing, and so are the factors that define successful sales strategies. Countless alternatives are available from domestic and international suppliers, so customers are smarter, better informed and more independent. Customers seek expertise and knowledge from people like us. That's why today's sales professional should handle objections differently. You need to take a good look at where customer resistance is coming from and understand what the objection really is, instead of disregarding or dismissing customer concerns.

Since information, knowledge and experience are publicly available, companies are redefining their sales approach. Companies need loyal customers, brand ambassadors who fully embrace the solution and can't wait to tell everyone about it, instead of complaining customers that shouldn't have been your target audience in the first place. What does that mean for you? The sales professional is no longer just responsible for selling those products. Instead, your top priority needs to be delivering value.

WHY ARE CUSTOMERS PLAYING HARD TO GET?

Selling is not always easy. On many occasions, customers just won't budge. They dig in, refuse to give an inch, and everything you try feels like a dead end. Knowing that every healthy sales cycle will include obstacles to overcome, the main question is not how to avoid them, but how to deal with them as they arise. As a sales professional, you shouldn't be focused on how each obstacle might affect your success rates. Instead, take a closer look from the customer's perspective, identifying what's driving customer resistance here. Selling isn't about being nice or cracking a couple jokes; a sales professional needs to be aware of the deeper dimensions involved here. Once you realize what's really bothering your customer, you can address the underlying issue and move forward.

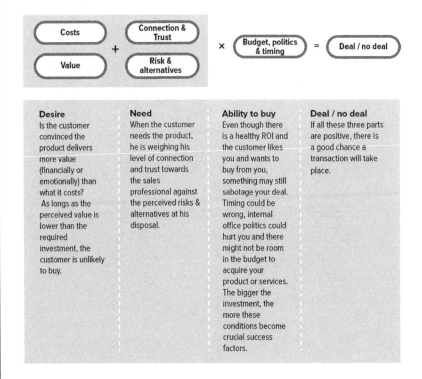

Desire
Is the customer convinced the product delivers more value (financially or emotionally) than what it costs? As longs as the perceived value is lower than the required investment, the customer is unlikely to buy.

Need
When the customer needs the product, he is weighing his level of connection and trust towards the sales professional against the perceived risks & alternatives at his disposal.

Ability to buy
Even though there is a healthy ROI and the customer likes you and wants to buy from you, something may still sabotage your deal. Timing could be wrong, internal office politics could hurt you and there might not be room in the budget to acquire your product or services. The bigger the investment, the more these conditions become crucial success factors.

Deal / no deal
If all these three parts are positive, there is a good chance a transaction will take place.

OBJECTIONS ACCORDING TO THE WOLF

Every objection just means you should push harder.

Look, when I start selling something, customers are always resistant. Of course they are. Their objections are just a way of showing me what they need from me before we can do business. I always say: objections are good, because it means they're engaging with me. A sale starts with lots of NOs. I just have to push forward; as long as I'm still in dialogue with the customer, I have a chance to sell. If I hear a NO, I need to flat-out ignore it, or attack the objection until I've convinced the customer I'm right. I just need to push harder than the customer can defend. I am not obnoxious; that's such a negative term! I prefer to say I'm persistent.

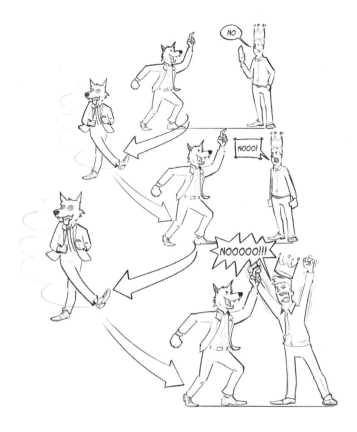

OBJECTIONS ACCORDING TO THE DOG

Every objection means you should re-align your approach.

Objections are customer responses that keep the sales professional at bay. The customer might be reluctant to share information, doesn't understand the topic sufficiently, doesn't want to forward my call to a colleague, or won't agree to book a demo, make an appointment or hear my proposal. Every time I encounter an objection, it means I need to reassess the situation. In hindsight, maybe I moved too fast, wasn't clear enough, or focused on the wrong aspect. I need to stay calm, catch my breath, and decide how to get back on the same level as my customer. Some objections are legitimate reasons to terminate the selling process, while others are simply minor obstacles that can be resolved. My goal is to review the objection critically with the customer. If further analysis shows that it makes sense to stop here, there's no point in pushing. In that case, I'd rather spend my time on other opportunities. You wouldn't insist on removing someone's appendix if they'd had it taken out last year, right? Let's go where we're needed.

DMU* ACCORDING TO THE WOLF

Speak to the person who signs the contract; the rest are just pawns.

There is nothing more frustrating than some low-ranking manager who won't share information and claims to be responsible for a project, but doesn't actually have any authority. If they can't sign, why I am even talking to them? These morons never tell the truth. I send my quote and then it's just radio silence. I can't even reach them after that. Ridiculous! Now I just demand to speak to the general manager from the start, because they're going to end up making the decision anyway. What a pain! Those pawns at the bottom never let me through; they're just wasting my time because they're too scared to escalate. Just cut out the middleman, go for gold. Waiting for low-level managers to sign is pointless. If I aim too low, I can kiss that deal goodbye – and I'm here to win!

*(DMU = Decision Making Unit, all the employees in a company who are involved in the buying process, from the consultant, expert, purchaser, user and director all the way up to the CEO

DMU ACCORDING TO THE DOG

Everyone involved in evaluating a purchase is important.

Lots of decisions are a group effort these days; everyone plays a role. I want to include all the stakeholders so we can be sure the project will succeed. Everyone's important to the process! I want to understand each person's views, goals, interests and opinions so I know my quote will be feasible and meet the company's needs after implementation. It's not just about the person who ultimately signs off on the project; if the warehouse manager is the end user, I need to understand what's important to him too. Somehow, I always manage to talk to other key managers, departments and relevant people; it's a natural part of my process. Stakeholder involvement is second nature. The funny thing is, I rarely see my competitors doing the same thing.

Convincing according to the wolf

Customers are greedy, status-sensitive, social animals who copycat all the time. It doesn't really matter what you try, as long as it works.

I always say: 'all is fair in love and war ...and sales!' Customers are most inclined to buy when they think they're getting a great deal. I've developed the perfect way to convince them: tell them that all the top companies in their industry are using it, but it's almost sold out. Limited access boosts interest. If they're still being difficult, tell them that if they don't move fast, they'll miss out on affordable rates. Say that prices will be going up soon, but you're willing to give them an exclusive discount, just this once. The fact that you actually spiked prices by 50% before offering the 'discount' will be our little secret... Customers are greedy and offering discounts can work wonders. Another trick I use is telling customers that all their main competitors are also doing business with us and they wouldn't want to miss out. Spice the sauce by mentioning that failure to choose me, the clear market leader, will mean his manager will get mad at him... And he'd deserve it, too! What a dope.

Convincing According to the Dog

Customers seek value, the right supplier and the right investment.
Prove that and you have a customer for life.

I wouldn't have sent the proposal if I wasn't 100% sure that this product is genuinely right for the customer. After receiving the proposal, some customers may have doubts. Logical, right? It's only human. Especially on large-scale or long-term projects, these decisions aren't made casually. It's important to talk to the customer and really understand why they're hesitating. If I don't check with them, I'm not just risking the deal; I may also be risking potential loss of value for the customer. Although I'm loyal to my customers, that doesn't mean I'm not assertive, nor that I won't fight for what's important. I don't make that effort for what the customer thinks they want – I do it for what I know they need. I love to have a healthy debate about that distinction with my customers. All the arguments I bring to the table are from the customer's perspective, because by now I know the customer really well. That extra effort often provides the confirmation that the customer needs in this phase, that last little push to make the right decision.

93

DEAL OR NO DEAL

We all know the type: the stereotypical salesman who tries to outsmart you just to make a deal, using lazy tricks in an attempt to manipulate you. You know the excuses: Prices will go up next month! We've only got 4 left so you should buy now! It's just a couple hundred bucks a month, so it's a steal! I can't hold the product much longer for you.

Customers are becoming less naive, and they are less and less susceptible to 'now-or-never' strategies. It gets worse, too: customers who are tricked into buying are much less likely to be satisfied with what you're selling them. It's actually counterproductive to sign up the wrong customers and rack up those negative reviews. You're risking payment issues, negative comments on social media, and exponentially increasing customer service costs as your company vainly tries to squeeze a triangle in a square.

There's a better way to negotiate: shift your focus from price to value. Customers aren't deciding to buy based solely on price. The best approach is simple: look at the value that the product represents and explain why it's legitimately a good deal from the customer's perspective. You'll kill two birds with one stone: you get to close the deal and satisfy another customer, and you won't need any tricks to get it done.

A GAME OF TRUST

"It takes 20 years to build a reputation and five minutes to ruin it."

Warren Buffet is so right. The beauty of it is, wolves have to keep jumping through hoops just to avoid being caught out, while dogs are trustworthy by nature and will be consistent in whatever they do. The higher the risk involved a possible contract, the more important trust becomes. Your buyer will consider various factors in deciding whether he trusts enough to sign. Does he trust the person he's buying from? Does he trust the product will add the right value? Even more importantly: does he trust that you will be the right supplier for his company? That sense of possible exposure becomes more apparent when dealing with bigger companies. If the buyer chooses the wrong supplier, it could have consequences for his job, so buyers will avoid those complications at all cost. Trust is relatively easy to earn, but you can lose your customer's trust in a split second if you're not conscientious.

Dogs:
- Always honor commitments;
- Are honest and up-front if something isn't not possible, needs to be changed, or will be delayed;
- Won't make promises that they or their organization can't keep;
- Are consistent in how they communicate and what they do.
-

Wolves:
- Rarely honor anything and are always looking for the short-cuts and taking the easy way out;
- Tell the customer what they want to hear, digging themselves into a hole;
- Make promises they know they and the organization can't keep;
- Are inconsistent in how they communicate and act towards the customer.

Negotiating According to the Wolf

*Price wars all around! In negotiations,
force the customer to commit on pricing before anything else.*

It is a tough world out there. Customers always want low prices, and then demand that I go even lower. No matter how big a discount I offer, they keep nagging to get more out of the deal. I just stay firm as long as I can. I also try to intimidate them into thinking I might back out, revoke my offer. Or I go for the guilt trip, telling them about how hard I worked to get this great deal for them and how scared I am that I'll lose my job if it doesn't get signed. When it comes down to it, all I really want is the deal, since that's what my commission is based on, so I'll go ahead even if it's not the best price for my company. If my boss starts complaining, I'll just tell him we're too expensive, even if the company is losing money on the deal. Who cares, as long as I rope this customer in – literally. All I care about is what I'm getting out of it. Let the money roll, baby!

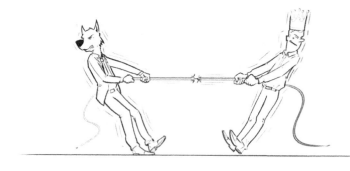

NEGOTIATING ACCORDING TO THE DOG

Seek the highest possible value for both parties,
making a healthy deal that will grow over time.

Negotiating is a logical part of the buying process. My main concern is understanding why the customer is negotiating. Is it a budget issue? Does the person want to show their boss that they know how to negotiate? Do I need to put more effort into demonstrating value? Each reason requires a different response and an appropriate approach. Since value for my customer is central to the agreement, I know what the benefits are, so I know how much I can realistically knock off the price – and whether I really need to. I'm primarily focused on securing value for the customer, at a price he accepts and is willing to pay. Achieving balance between these elements maximizes my chances of building a valuable relationship.

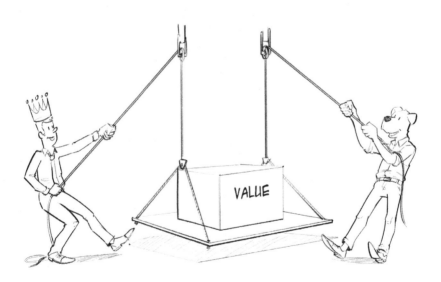

Closing the Deal According to the Wolf

Always try to close the deal; getting it sold is the only priority.

ABC — Always Be Closing! As a natural born salesman, I always seek the signature, the thrill of the deal. The rest is pure distraction. Sure, I guess customers want to know stuff, but I don't really care about those petty details. It's all just background noise to me. I give customers just enough attention to convince them, and then I go for the kill. I'm great at getting them to sign. I just tell them that the deal on the table is the best there is. I love exaggerating or making up stories, anything I can do to trick the customer into signing. Closing deals gives me such a kick; it's a wonderful rush. If you're not addicted to the adrenaline of that moment, you don't belong in sales. It is as simple as that. Like world-class sports or the dating game, competition is everywhere, and scoring a deal is the be-all and end-all of doing business. What happens afterwards is irrelevant, because I won't be around to see it anyway. I'll be working on my next deal!

CLOSING THE DEAL ACCORDING TO THE DOG

Always try to open the deal; securing customer value is top priority.

No contract means no delivery, no improvement, no added value – the deal's not the point. It just marks the start of a new phase. Once the deal is on the table, it's time for both parties to sign. If there's any sense of urgency, it's not about the signature, it's about the urgent need to get the product to the customer. Delivery or implementation is their main priority, not the deal! Once we reach this point, the customer is often in more of a hurry than I am. They're eager to sign so we can start implementation. There's no need to push them to sign; if they still need to be convinced at that point in the process, then I haven't done my job right. Customers who are pushed into signing are much more likely to be dissatisfied; it's a complete waste of time. As far as I'm concerned, the high point of the sales process is that moment when the customer starts enjoying the product. Customers you can grow with together is what I'm really aiming for.

THE CONTRACT ACCORDING TO THE WOLF

Get the signature, count your money, and get out as fast as you can.

I prefer not to discuss the contents of the contract. My response to most questions is that it is standard policy at our company. I'll claim that every customer signs this contract and there's no need to discuss the default terms and conditions. Just check the box and sign on the dotted line, thankyouverymuch. The moment the contract gets signed is just amazing, especially when I can actually see the pen moving over the paper. It gives me such a feeling of power. What a moron! I would never sign this contract, especially on these terms, haha. That's just how good I am; I can convince anyone to buy, and closing the deal on this customer just confirms I'm great at sales. I especially love it when I can convince people to sign up for more than they were planning. I always make sure to ask for recommendations as soon as the deal is closed. That's the time to generate new leads, because I know they'll never come back if I wait for them to take the initiative. It's a hard, cold world out there, and there's no loyalty or repeat business. It's now or never!

THE CONTRACT ACCORDING TO THE DOG

The contract should cover all the details. Avoid confusion and create clarity.

I want to make sure that the company delivers the right product in the right way and at the right time, exactly as the contract states. No unpleasant surprises, please! That's why it's so important to ensure that the contract protects both parties and states the terms as clearly as possible. Before signing, I run through a quick summary with my customer to make sure we're on the same page for the options, terms and conditions, and possible scenarios, so we both know all the ins and outs of the actual transaction. Once the contract is signed, I always take time to celebrate it with my customer. It's an important opportunity, because this shared moment is when customers often voluntarily share useful ideas, referrals and contacts.

After-Sales

If you're always promising too much, you'll never exceed expectations. It's better to make realistic promises so you can do your best to overdeliver. That's how you impress your customers! The customer experience needs to be even better than expected. By the time the product has been delivered and implemented, the customer should be pleasantly surprised every step of the way. This not only creates maximum customer satisfaction, but also transforms your customers into active brand ambassadors, telling everyone how much they loved your company and how great you were. That's how you establish your reputation as a sales professional. There's no need to beg for introductions if your customers are singing your praises to everyone they meet. When referrals become a constant flow, new contacts and opportunities will come your way left, right and center. Not because you're the type of sales professional who goes out there and claims it to get attention and boost results, but because you've earned it.

Extremely satisfied customers don't just grow on trees, of course. As a sales professional, you have a role to play and can influence customer perceptions, but it's still hard work. Once a project is completed successfully, the results affirm the customer's choice. Working with you was clearly a great idea, not because you said so, but because he's experienced the benefits first-hand. If project implementation was thorough and effective, your company has had numerous opportunities to work with the customer to identify new issues and figure out whether your other products and services might offer a solution. The customer knows you have his best interests at heart, so he'll be more than open to seriously discuss options and consider moving forward if there's still room for improvement.

THE SALES AMBASSADOR

A ny customer who's sufficiently convinced could easily become your ambassador. They're better than any publicity money could buy, and they'll go to great lengths on your behalf – without being asked, or asking for anything in return. It's fine to discuss this with your customer. If they're impressed with the entire experience, he'll be more than willing to harness the benefits of his business network and tell everyone how great you are. Disappointed customers, on the other hand, will not only decline to share their network with you, but may well warn their network not to do business with you. It is even worse when a neglected customer goes out of his way to share his negative experiences online. Those angry customer reviews tend to linger, remaining available to the public for a long, long time – including all your potential new customers. No marketing campaign can completely erase the impact of a flood of negative reviews. If you can ensure the sales and delivery process is optimal throughout the customer engagement cycle, you'll create the perfect conditions to transform your customers into ambassadors.

What's the benefit of new potential customers getting in touch with your ambassadors?

- They trust ambassadors much more than sales professionals (once bitten, twice shy, and there's an awful lot of wolves out there).
- They see ambassadors as an objective source.
- They can hear first-hand what it's like to work with you as a sales professional.
- They instantly see that the product works well and satisfies customer expectations, so they're more likely to accept that it's good. After all, someone they trust said so!

This enhanced trust will accelerate the buying cycle and make it a lot easier to identify another perfect match. What does that mean for you? The more ambassadors you create, the more leads you'll get from your current customers – and the average buying cycles will be shorter, too. Let the wolves slog along in the muck; dogs are working on something much bigger that will last a lifetime... or longer.

Delivery According to the Wolf

The customer is solely responsible for the transaction; once I make the sale, I shouldn't have to care what happens after that.

I get it all the time: those pesky customer complaints. Look, the fact they said yes too fast and didn't bother considering all the factors well enough is not my problem. I just offered the product. That's it. The product may not work exactly the way it should or the way they expected it to, but hey, tough luck! It's their own fault. They're the ones who decided to sign; the price and the terms were right there in the fine print. I think customers are responsible for checking the facts themselves. Presenting background research on a silver platter isn't MY job. I wouldn't sell anything ever again if I actually had to warn my customers of the risks involved. I'd have to be crazy to practice full disclosure!

DELIVERY ACCORDING TO THE DOG

Sales is accountable for the transaction, ensuring value keeps being delivered as promised.

Beautiful, just beautiful! It's so amazing to see customers using the product exactly as intended and watching the predicted benefits blossom. This is when I like to take a moment to evaluate the process, assess the results, and see whether I can improve how I help other potential customers attain a similar positive impact. Regardless of what ended up on paper, I think it's vital to ensure that we delivered actual value. If it turns out after delivery that the choices we put in the contract weren't ideal, I first check to see whether I could have anticipated the problems. Even if it's caused by factors beyond my control, I try to see where we can be flexible. I'm keenly aware that delivering anything less than our very best poses a risk to customer loyalty – and anything that detracts from customer value is against my core principles. This is the moment of truth and the customer should be able to rest assured he made the right choice. I'm a worthy dog; the customer's trust was justified.

RELATIONSHIP ACCORDING TO THE WOLF

Boooooooring.

Relati-what now? What do you mean, relationship? I only work on contacts that give me money in the short term. I am here to sell; that's all I do. Managing customers isn't my responsibility. If that's what they're looking for, they should check with customer service.... unless they want to spend money, in which case I'm your guy. Or when a contract is about to expire. If a customer's interested in discussing the next deal, he should definitely talk to me, because I am soooooo customer-driven... Bye now, gotta go pretend to be really busy helping customers until a new prospect crosses my path!

RELATIONSHIP ACCORDING TO THE DOG

Keep nurturing the relationship.

I find it important to maintain my relationships to ensure I remain valuable to the customer. That is how I create loyalty. I keep in touch with my customers, even if they are not ready to purchase new products. I'm sure they'll need my guidance again, so it's vital not to start from scratch every time. Since I know my customer's company and sector, I can detect opportunities relatively quickly, so I already know whether they need our products. My customer knows I am their ideal partner to make the right choices, and they always appreciate my honest input. Sometimes my customers' co-workers are surprised to realize I'm a business partner rather than part of their company. That is one of the nicest compliments I can get!

NETWORKING ACCORDING TO THE WOLF

Everyone you meet is either a customer or a distraction.

I am on the prowl. No matter where I go, I'm always scanning the audience and looking for the most important people. Like so much in sales, it's a numbers game. At a networking event, or any event for that matter, I skim from one person to another. Why would I waste my time on boring bystanders who won't buy my products anyway? I look for big fat customers, the head honchos in any setting, and try to schmooze them. I buddy up, laugh along with their jokes, show my business card as quickly as possible so they'll be impressed and respect me. If there's any time at all, I try to score a meeting. These guys are business-savvy too, so they won't be surprised that I'm trying to work the situation to my advantage. I'll ask if they can recommend any customers; everyone wants to help out, right? Why not give them a chance? :-) Most people get all awkward when I ask them about leads, but hey – sometimes it works out, and then I'm in. Boom! Another name to chase down. Selling never stops; let's rock!

NETWORKING ACCORDING TO THE DOG

Everyone you meet is a chance to discover value.

Networking is fantastic! I love having that opportunity to meet new people and see how we can help each other. I like helping others to be successful, because that can lead to new contacts that I might never have considered. Networking isn't about direct selling, it's about building business relationships and friendships. We exchange ideas and experiences and discover mutual new opportunities. The more I invest in my network, the more I get back – but that's not why I do it. The more active I am in networking with people, the more I get introduced to new and interesting individuals, the more spontaneous opportunities I discover. The best new connections often come from unexpected places in unexpected ways.

The Dog and the Wolf in the Sales Professional

Looking at the sales dilemmas that sales professionals face on a daily basis, it is never as black and white as this book portrays. It is important to realize that no sales professional is ever 100% dog or 100% wolf when interacting with customers. Remember that these two styles have been exaggerated to clarify the contrast. It's also important not to assume that everything a wolf does is bad and everything a dog does is good. Reality is a lot subtler, and often involves a mixture of both – and that's not necessarily a bad thing.

The wolf and dog actually have a lot to learn from each other. The wolf can learn that he doesn't have to be a money-grubbing loudmouth; wolves can achieve much more by understanding the customer's business better and showing more empathy. The dog can learn to avoid being too flexible and accommodating, giving in to everything a customer wants; dogs could benefit from playfully challenging the line without crossing it. Sometimes the customer needs some incentive or push-back to figure out what they really need and want.

Every choice you make in business defines who you are. It's time to look in the mirror and ask yourself that important question: Who do you want to be? Do you want to be the wolf or the dog? What would give you greater satisfaction? Wouldn't it be great if you could look back on a career that sets a great example for how business should be done? You should be able to look back with pride on how you did business and the way your choices benefit the environment and the world we live in, now and for generations to come.

What is the right way to sell? If you ask yourself what offers the most value for your customer without damaging the company you represent, the answer will often lead you in the right direction. You can start making better choices today!

Have you decided you'd like to become more professional and effective at being a sales dog? The right mindset is the first step to getting there. I'm pleased and proud to have the chance to contribute by offering the book before you. Once you fine-tune your mindset and reinforce the basic patterns, it's crucial to keep developing your dog skills as you go along: understand your customer's business, ask the right questions, address the real issues, and demonstrate simply and powerfully how you can help the customer move forward and be successful in his journey.

It is my sincere hope that this book will inspire you to make beautiful things happen with your customers, helping you to embrace your own vision and follow your own dream.

If you've made it this far, you're ready to start your journey towards becoming the ultimate sales dog. Follow the inspiration, and follow the fun! Build strong, healthy relationships with customers – not just because they like you, but because they know you're eager and willing to contribute. Don't let society, your customers' demands or your employer's expectations push you into being any less than you can be. Be the best sales professional out there by maximizing customer lifetime value. Go for it!

ABOUT THE AUTHOR

Yuri's passion for sales was ignited at Forrester Research, where he quickly became a consistent top performer. He has worked in sales for tech companies such as BT Global Services, where he landed large outsourcing deals.

His deep understanding of sales, combined with an innate ability to inspire, guide, and teach others, led to his training thousands of people across the globe over the past 12 years. Yuri's methodology of trust and value has resulted in unlocking the potential of countless of sales organizations to grow a sustainable portfolio of loyal customers.

He wrote this book, as an introduction to the game-changing Trust2Sales Model©, in order to inspire salespeople around the world to put trust and value at the heart of their sales processes. An ability to genuinely focus on the customer and earn their trust in a typically low-trust world allows sales professionals to rise above the noise and make a difference.

Master the 5 core principles of the Trust2Sales Model© by:
- Getting the free white paper (www.topsalesdogs.com)
- Claiming your first free course (www.topsalesdogs.com)
- Booking Yuri for your next sales event (www.yurivander.com)

Made in the USA
Columbia, SC
13 September 2018